AMERICAN SYMBOLS

Maria Koran

Go to **www.eyediscover.com** and enter this book's unique code.

BOOK CODE

AVP37428

EYEDISCOVER brings you optic readalongs that support active learning.

Published by AV² by Weigl
350 5th Avenue, 59th Floor New York, NY 10118
Website: www.eyediscover.com

Library of Congress Cataloging-in-Publication Data available on request

ISBN 978-1-7911-0812-0 (hardcover)

Printed in Guangzhou, China
1 2 3 4 5 6 7 8 9 0 23 22 21 20 19

072019
121818

Project Coordinator: John Willis
Designers: Mandy Christiansen and Sushant Deshpande

Weigl acknowledges Dreamstime, iStock, and Shutterstock as the primary image suppliers for this title.

EYEDISCOVER provides enriched content, optimized for tablet use, that supplements and complements this book. EYEDISCOVER books strive to create inspired learning and engage young minds in a total learning experience.

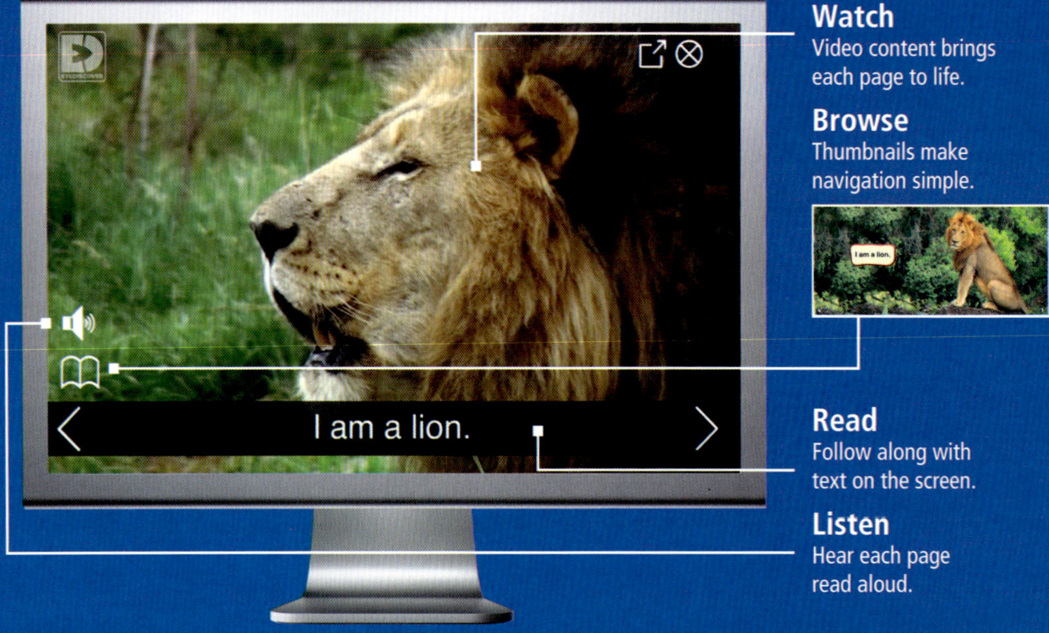

Watch
Video content brings each page to life.

Browse
Thumbnails make navigation simple.

Read
Follow along with text on the screen.

Listen
Hear each page read aloud.

Your EYEDISCOVER Optic Readalongs come alive with...

Audio
Listen to the entire book read aloud.

Video
High resolution videos turn each spread into an optic readalong.

OPTIMIZED FOR
- ✓ TABLETS
- ✓ WHITEBOARDS
- ✓ COMPUTERS
- ✓ AND MUCH MORE!

AMERICAN SYMBOLS

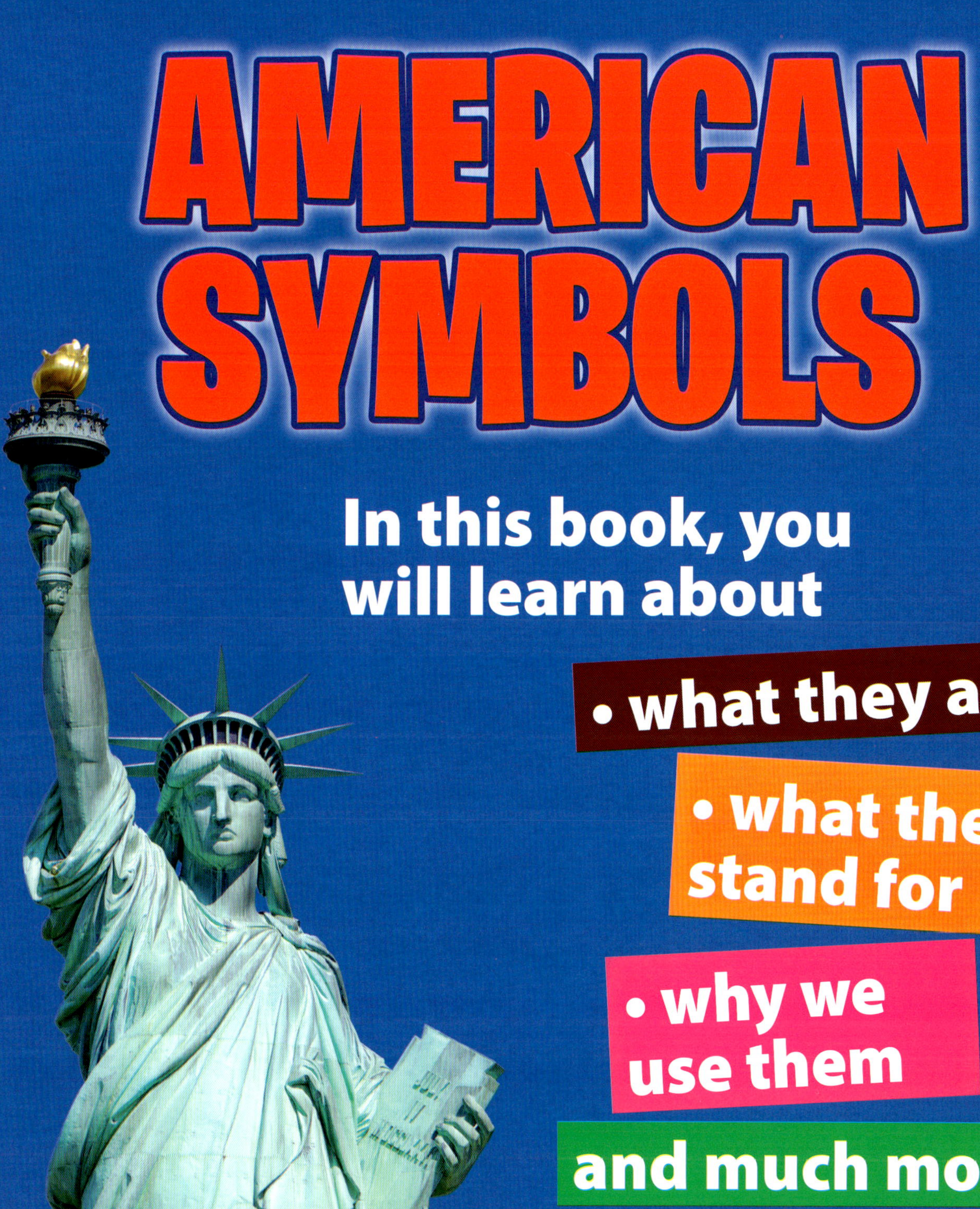

In this book, you will learn about

- **what they are**
- **what they stand for**
- **why we use them**

and much more!

The United States has many symbols. They help us remember America's values.

Independence Hall is where our country began. It reminds us of the hard work that made the United States.

The Capitol Building is a symbol of our laws. It reminds us of the ways we live and work together.

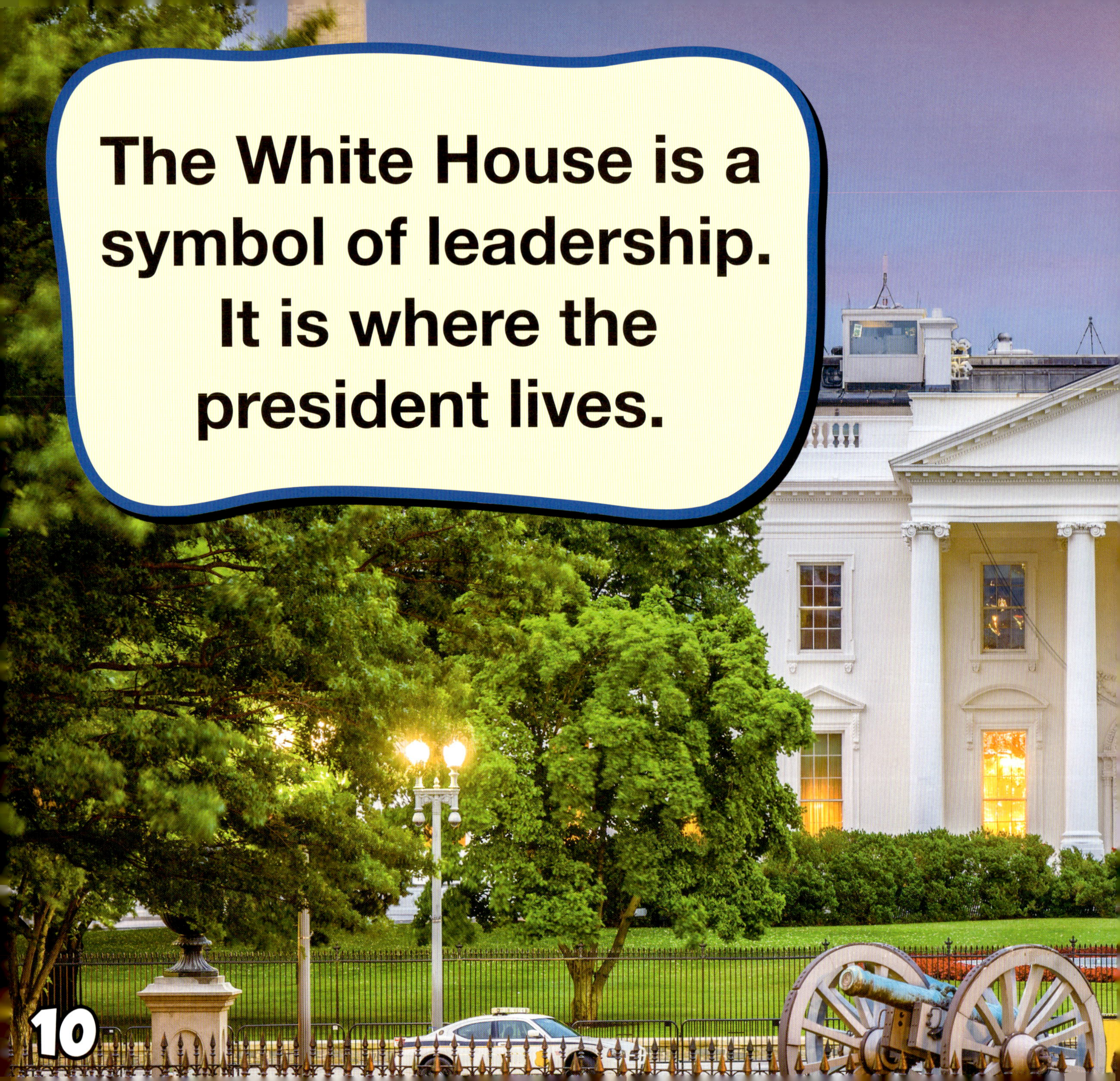

The White House is a symbol of leadership. It is where the president lives.

The Washington Monument honors George Washington. He led the United States to freedom.

The Jefferson Memorial reminds us of our freedoms. Thomas Jefferson helped write the Declaration of Independence.

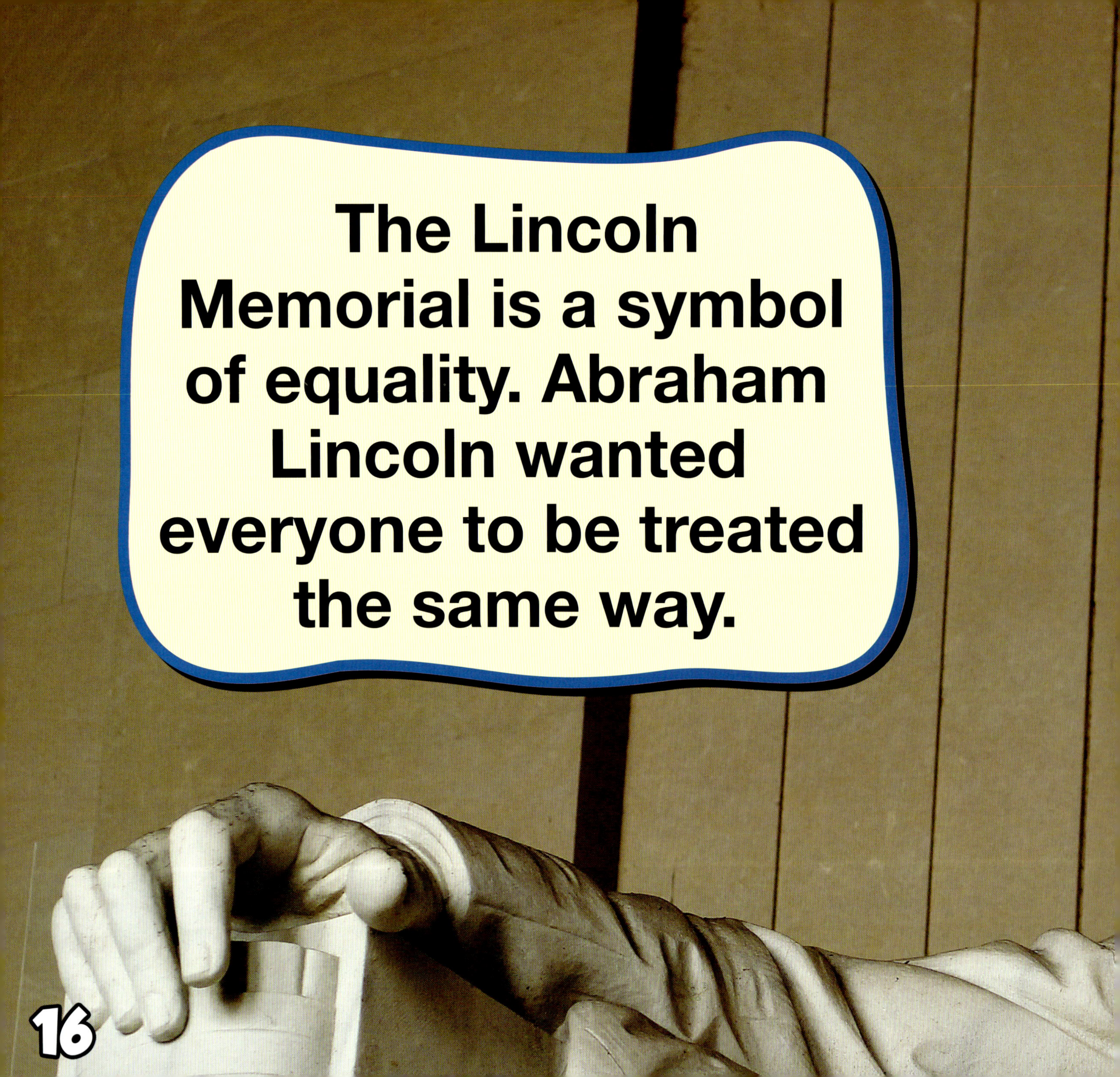

The Lincoln Memorial is a symbol of equality. Abraham Lincoln wanted everyone to be treated the same way.

The Statue of Liberty is a symbol of freedom. It welcomed people coming to America by boat.

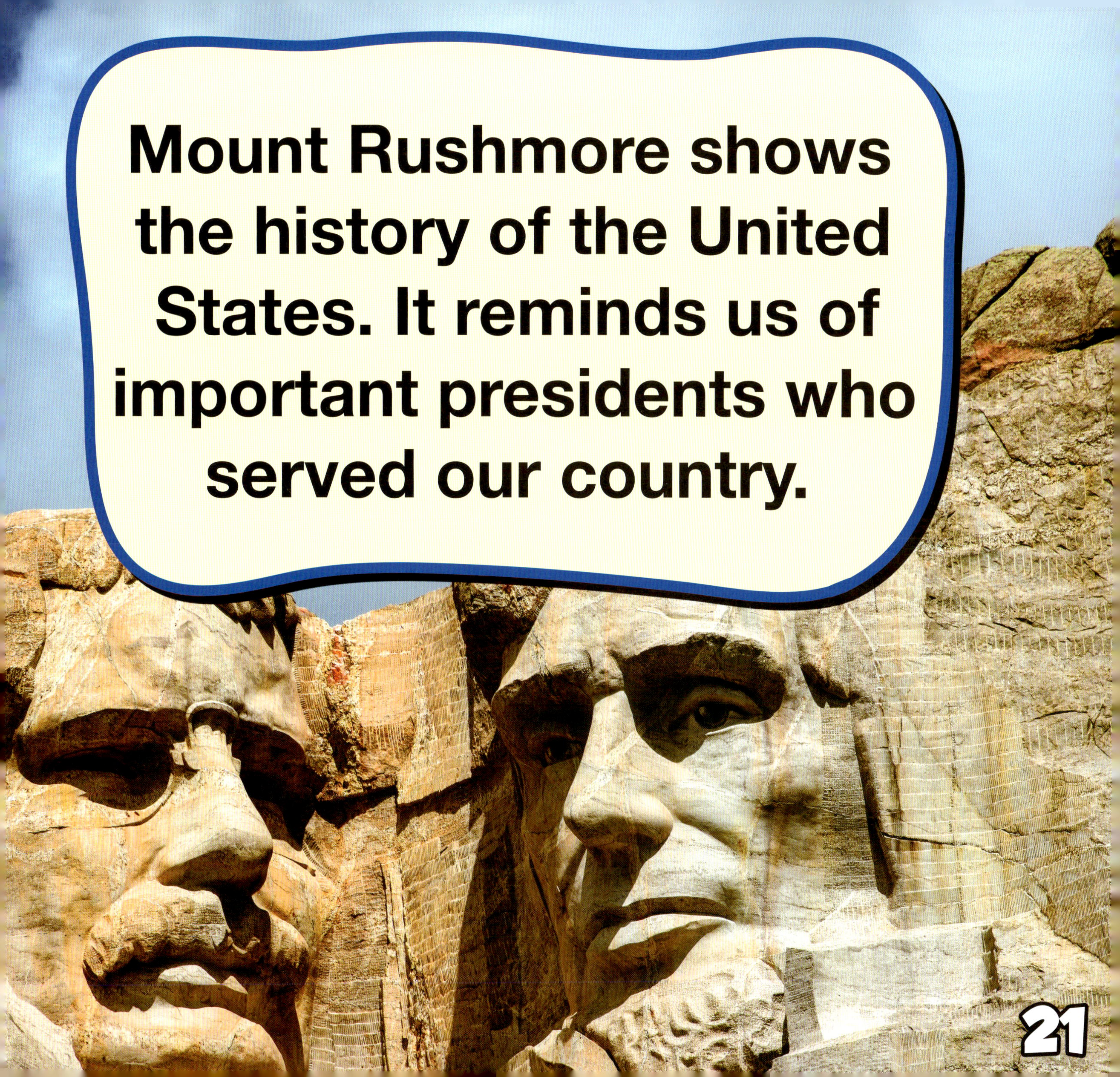

Mount Rushmore shows the history of the United States. It reminds us of important presidents who served our country.

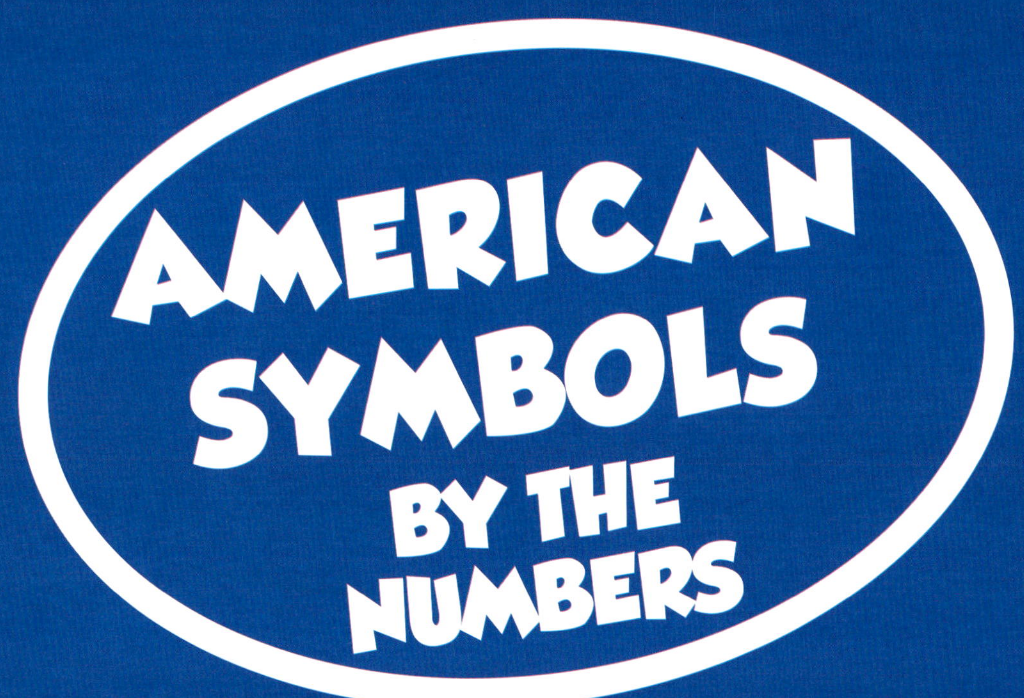

The **White House** has **132 rooms**.

The **Statue of Liberty** was a gift from **France** in **1884**.

Each face on **Mount Rushmore** is about **60 feet tall.**

(18.3 meters)

The **Washington Monument** weighs **91,000 tons.**

(82,554 metric tons)

The statue in the **Lincoln Memorial** is **19 feet tall.**

(5.8 meters)

KEY WORDS

Research has shown that as much as 65 percent of all written material published in English is made up of 300 words. These 300 words cannot be taught using pictures or learned by sounding them out. They must be recognized by sight. This book contains 39 common sight words to help young readers improve their reading fluency and comprehension. This book also teaches young readers several important content words, such as proper nouns. These words are paired with pictures to aid in learning and improve understanding.

Page	Sight Words First Appearance
5	America, are, has, help, many, state, the, they, us, used
6	began, country, hard, is, it, made, of, our, that, where, work
9	a, and, live, together, ways, we
10	house, white
13	he, to
15	write
16	be, same
18	by, people
21	important, shows, who

Page	Content Words First Appearance
5	symbols, United States, values
6	Independence Hall
9	Capitol Building, laws
10	leadership, president, White House
13	freedom, George Washington, Washington Monument
15	Declaration of Independence, Jefferson Memorial, Thomas Jefferson
16	Abraham Lincoln, equality, Lincoln Memorial
18	boat, Statue of Liberty
21	history, Mount Rushmore

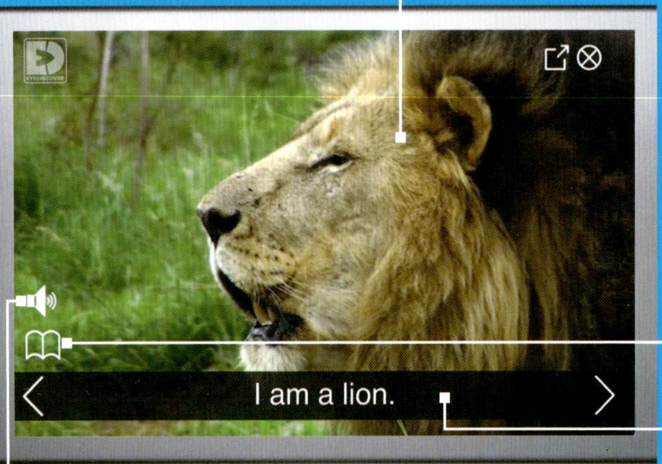

Watch
Video content brings each page to life.

Browse
Thumbnails make navigation simple.

Read
Follow along with text on the screen.

Listen
Hear each page read aloud.

Go to www.eyediscover.com and enter this book's unique code.

BOOK CODE

AVP37428